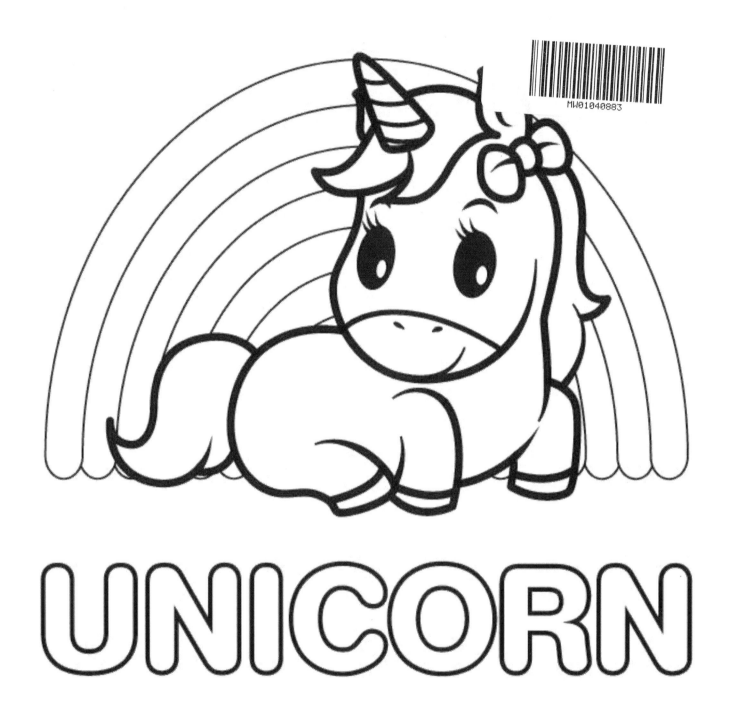

# UNICORN

## This Coloring Book Belongs to :

...................................................

...................................................

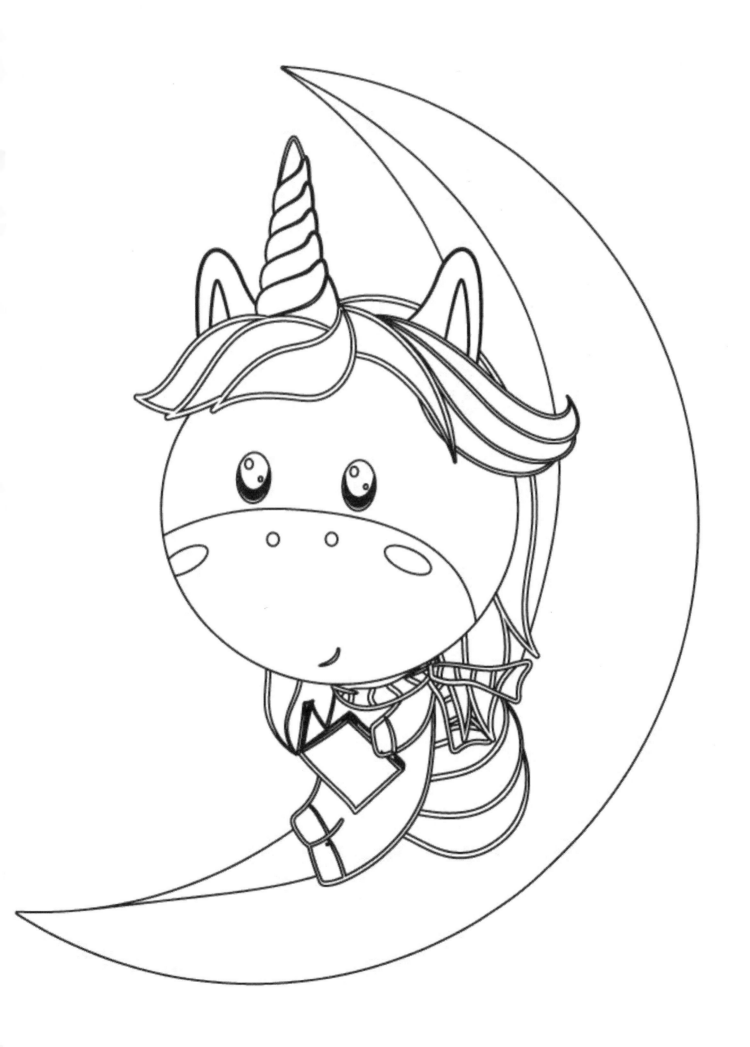

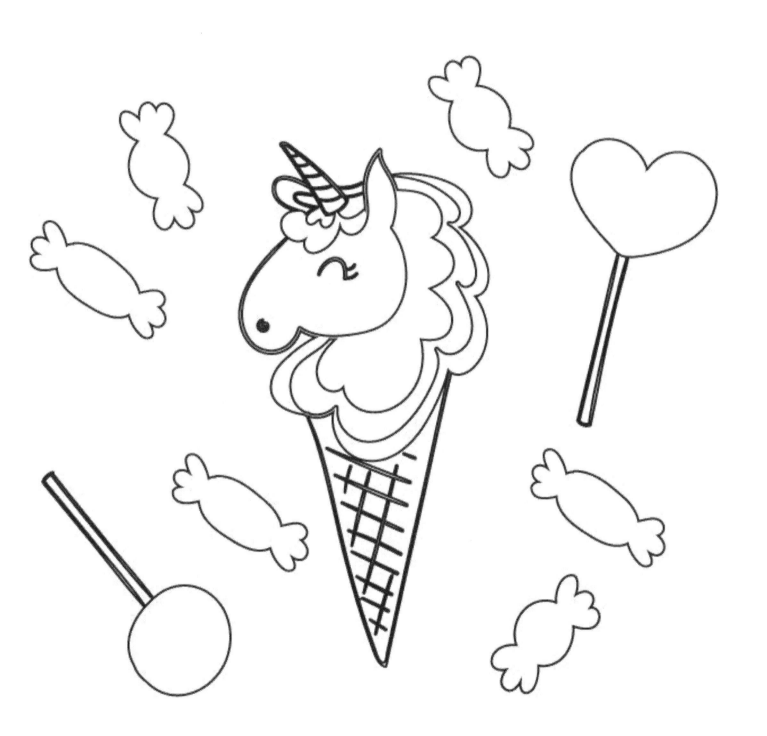

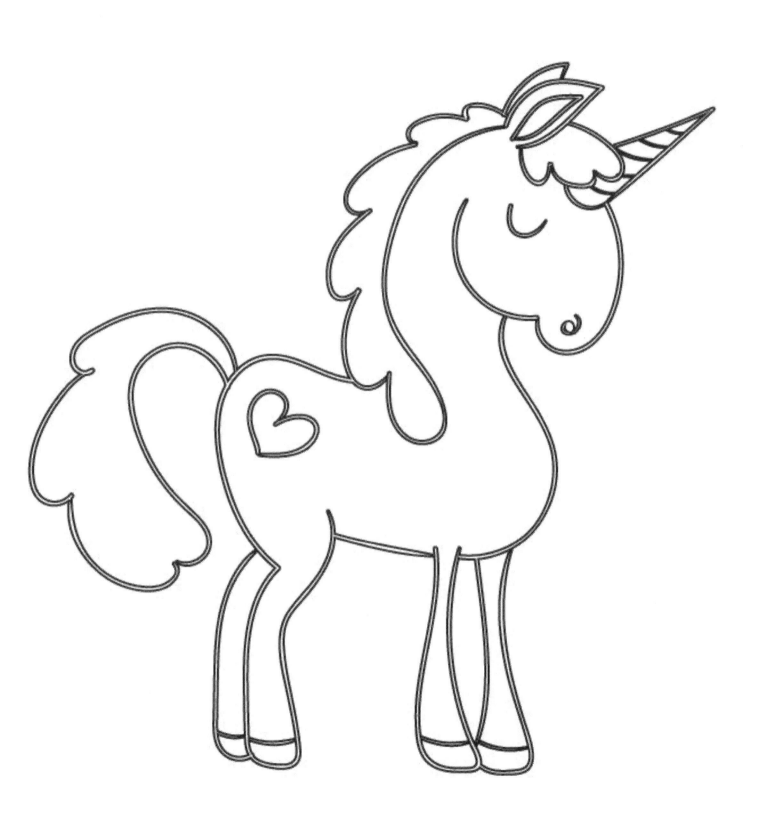

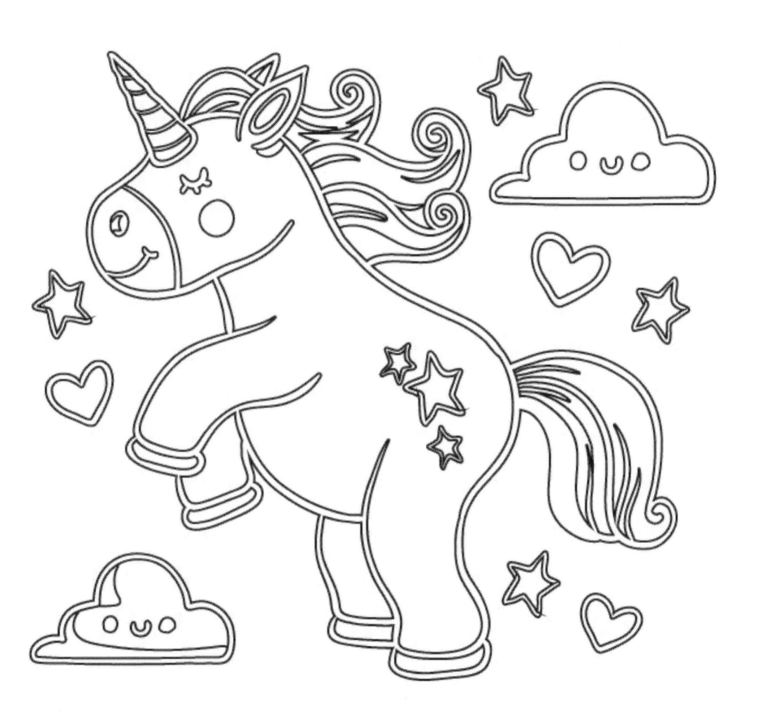

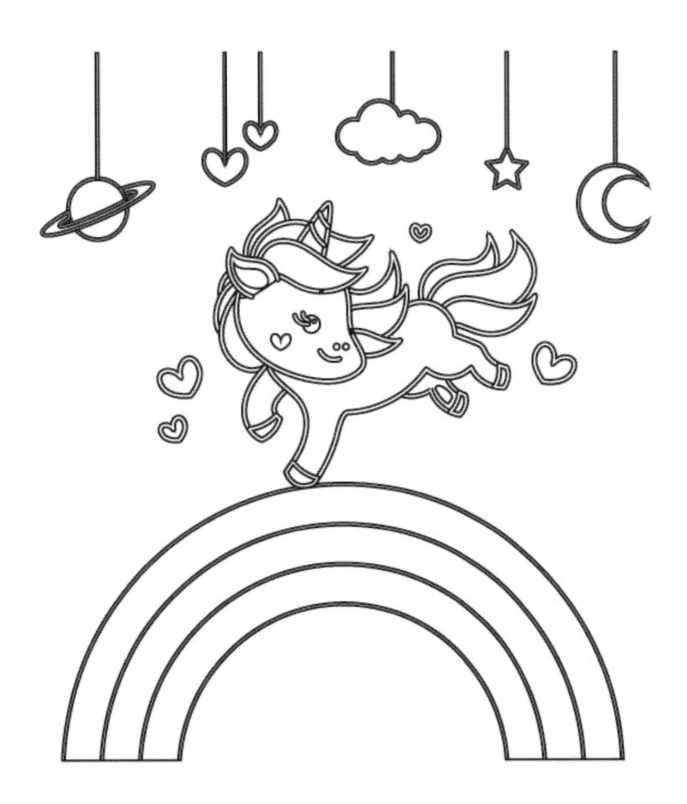

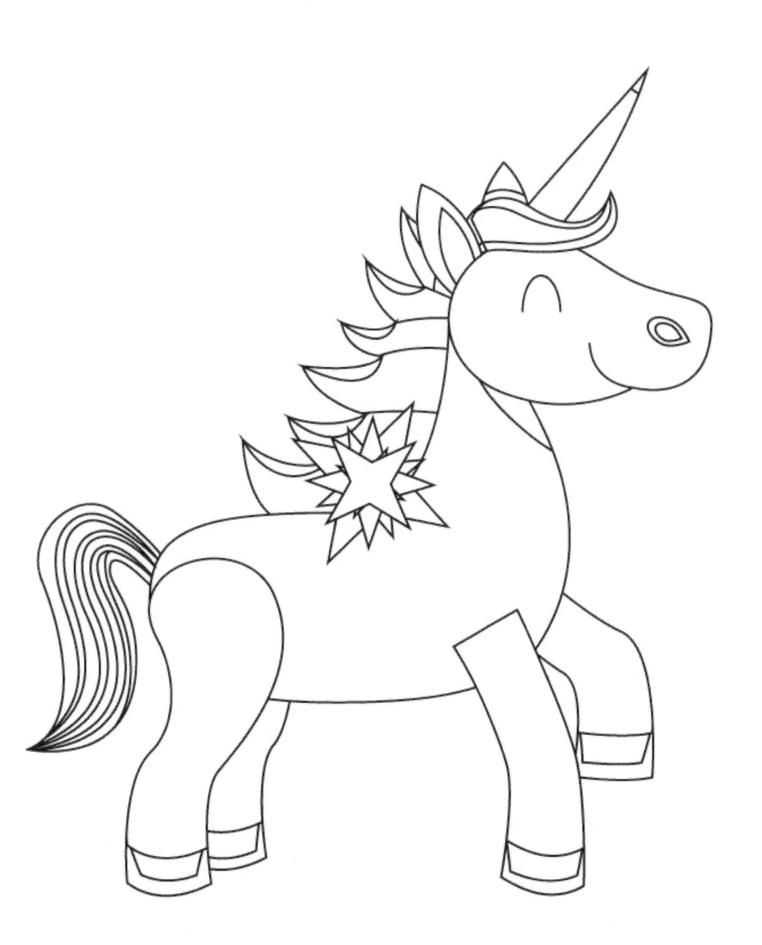

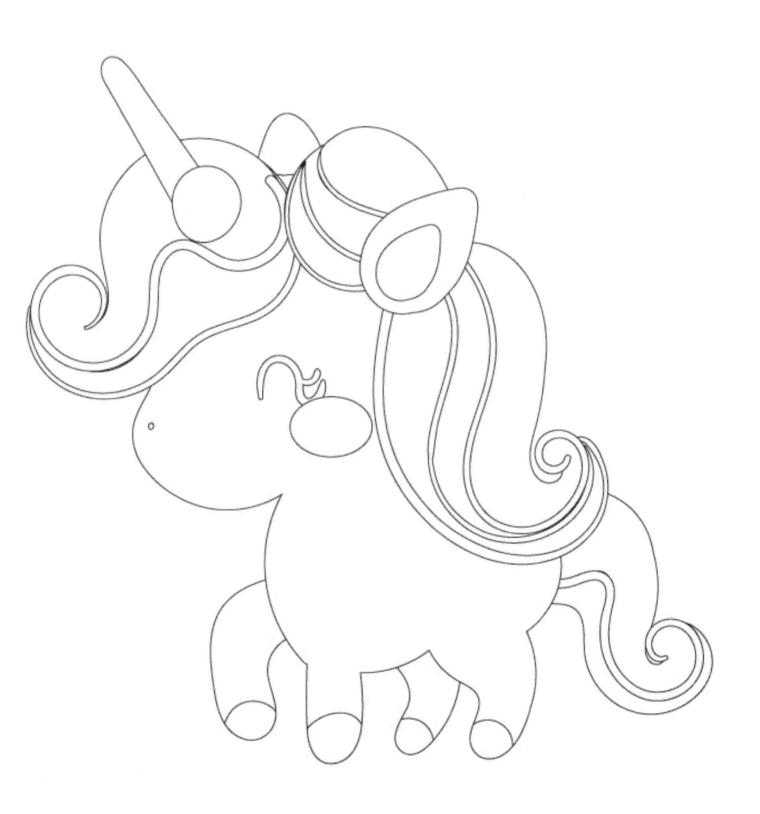

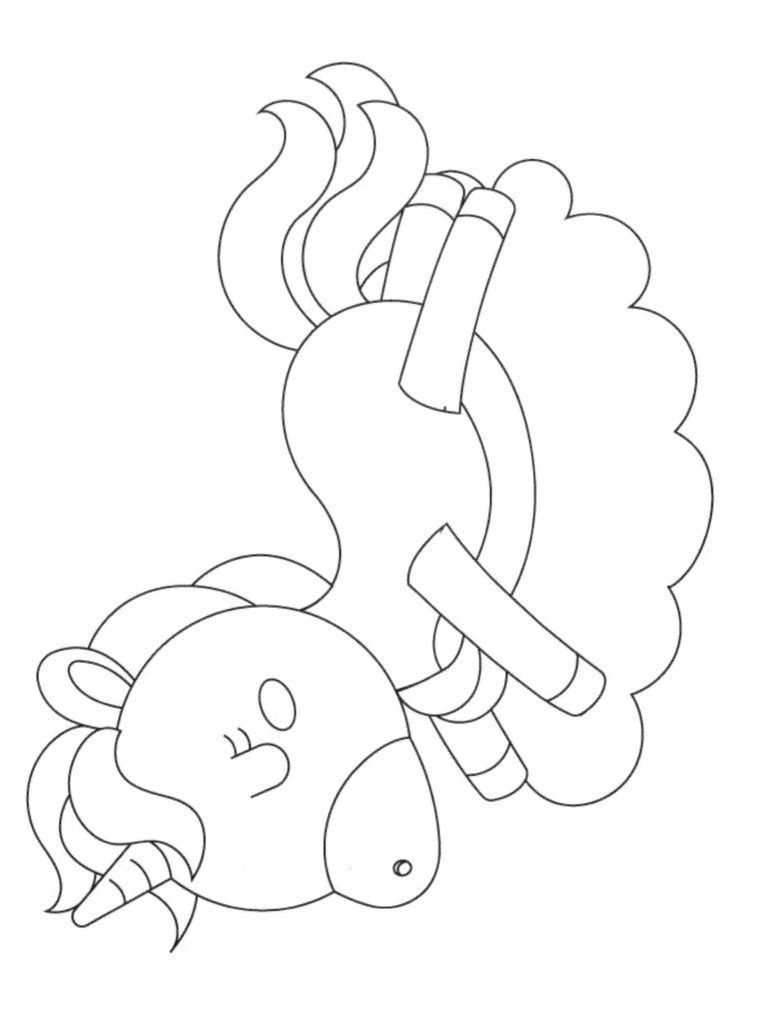

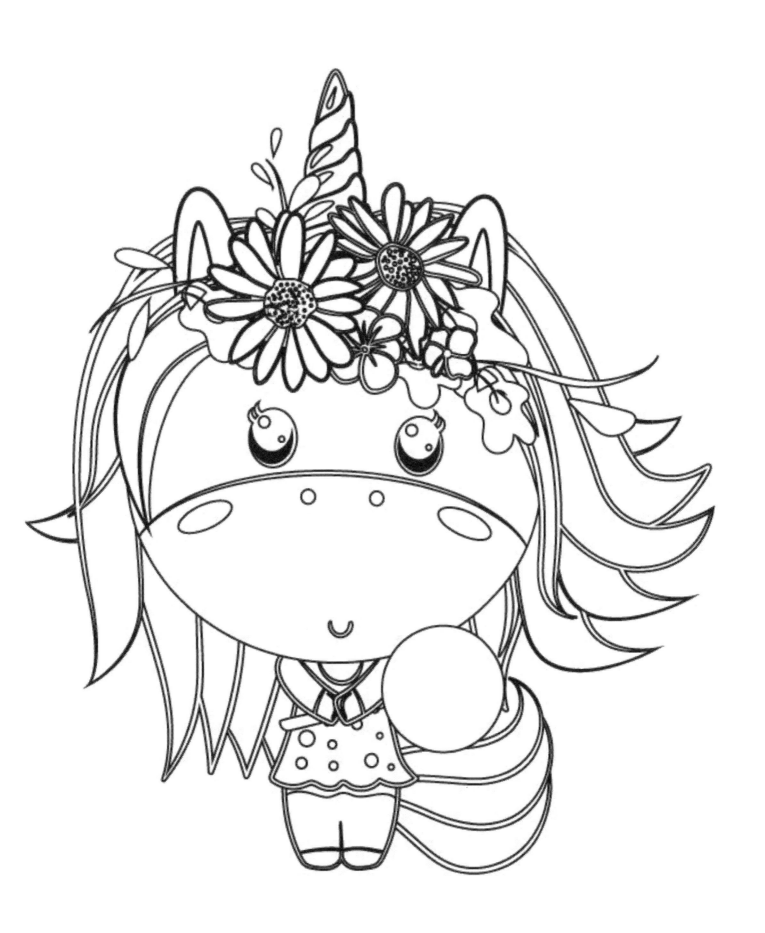

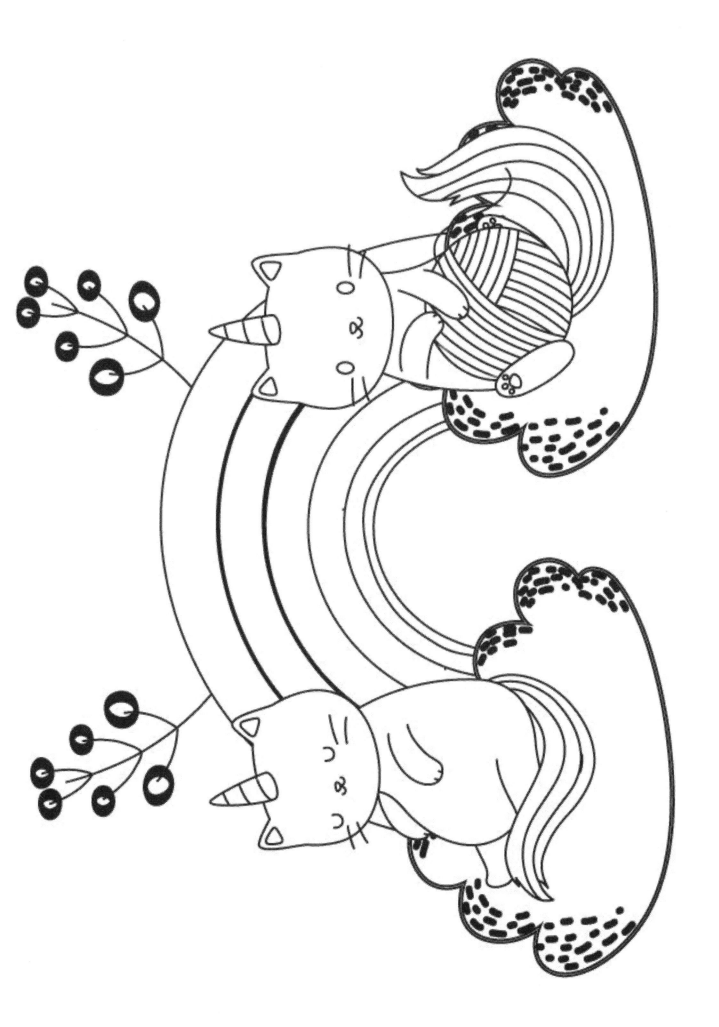

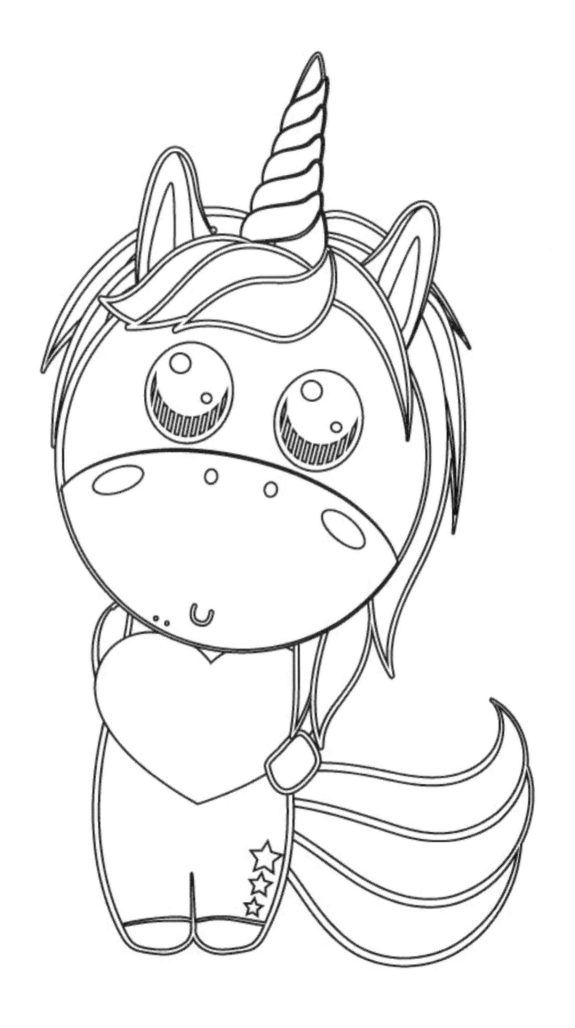

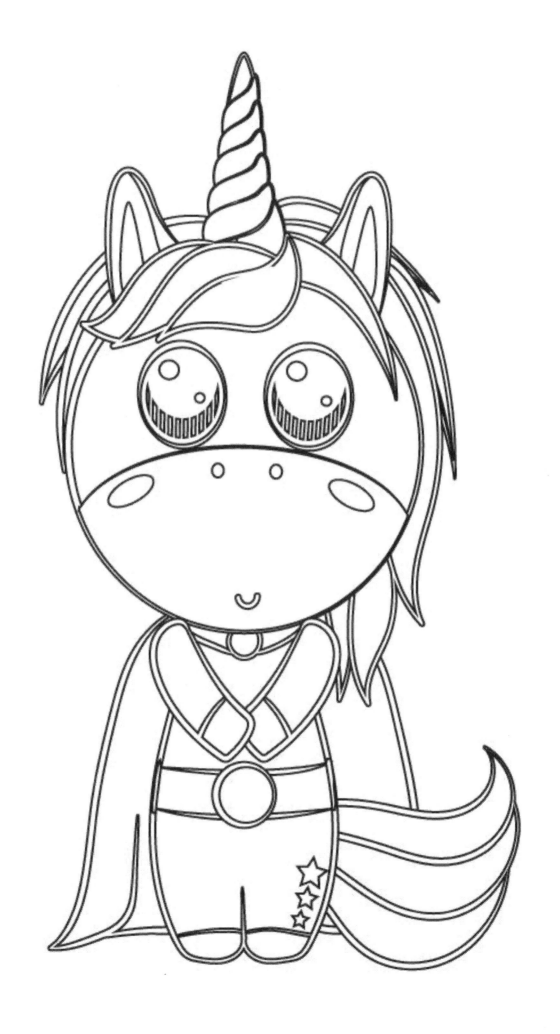

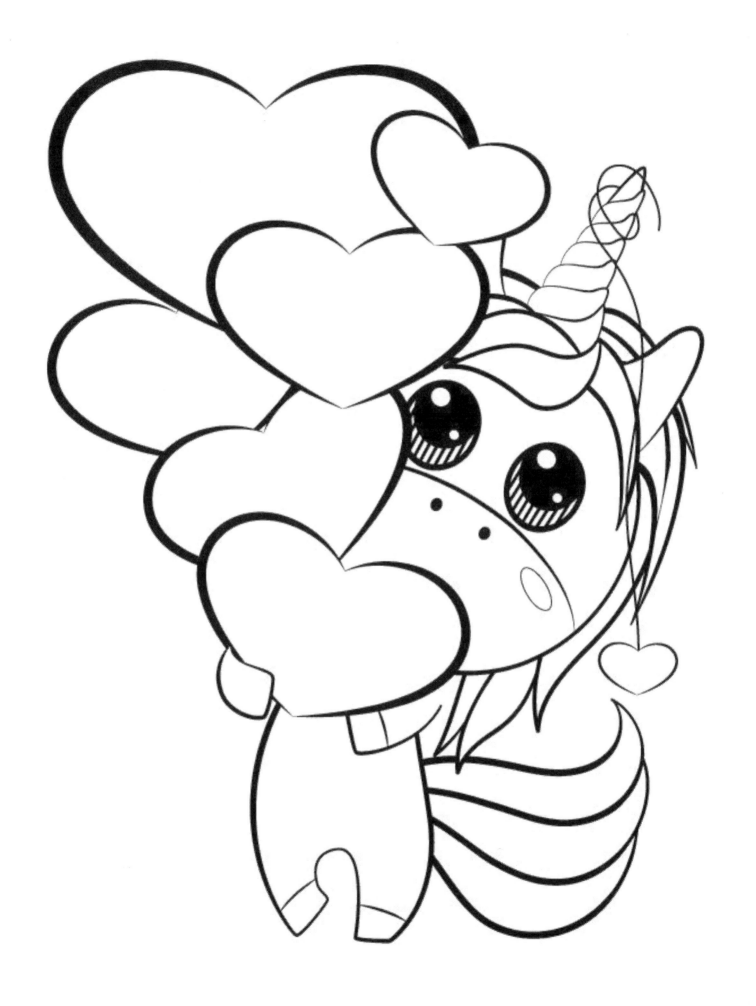

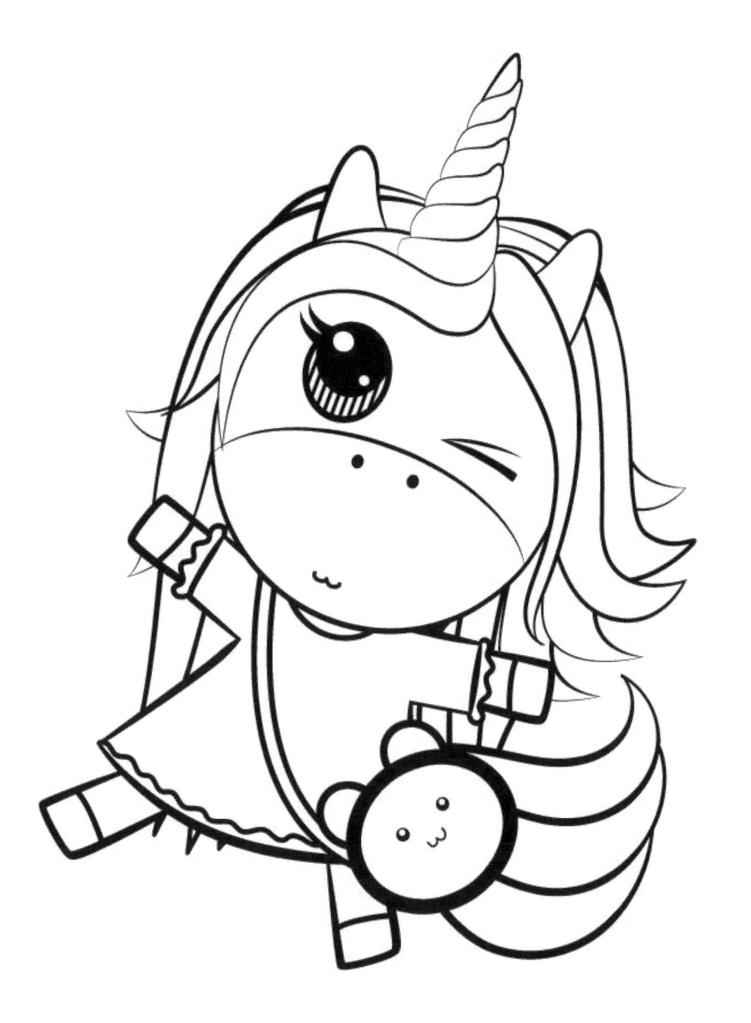

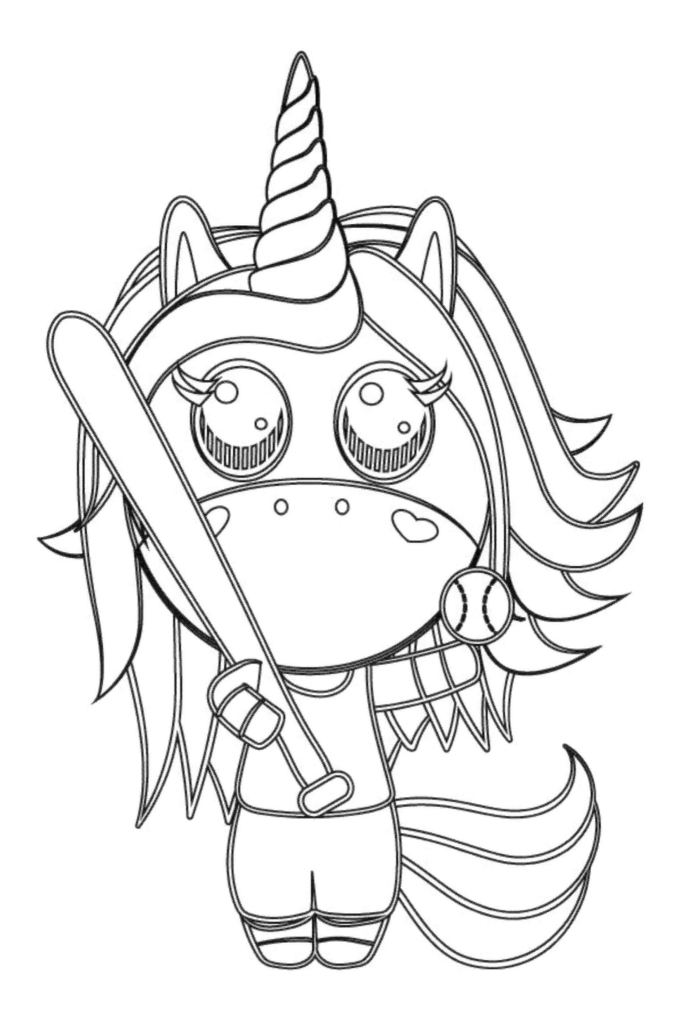

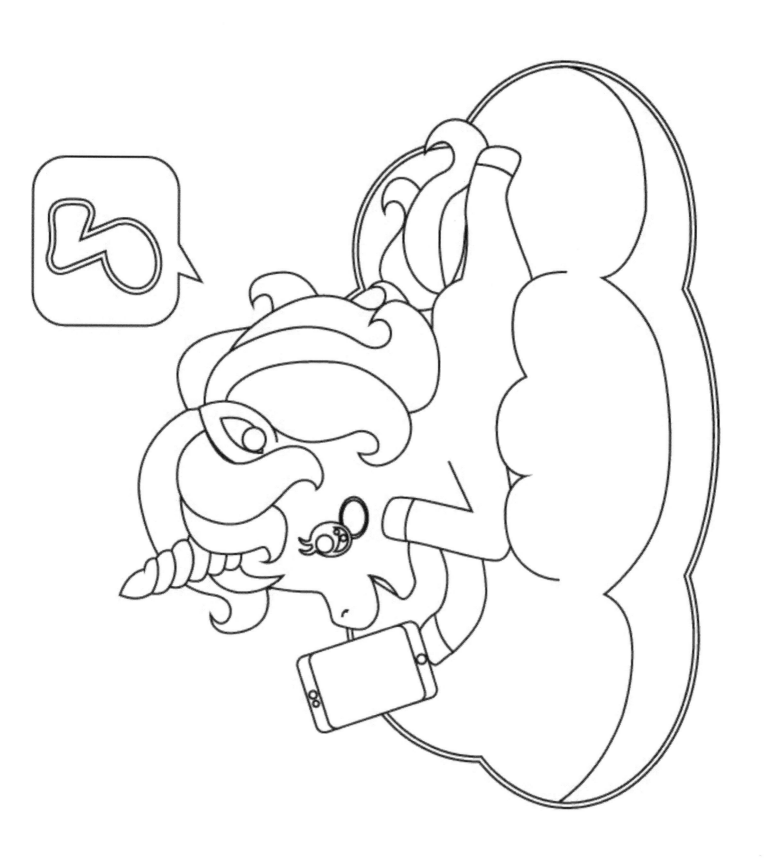

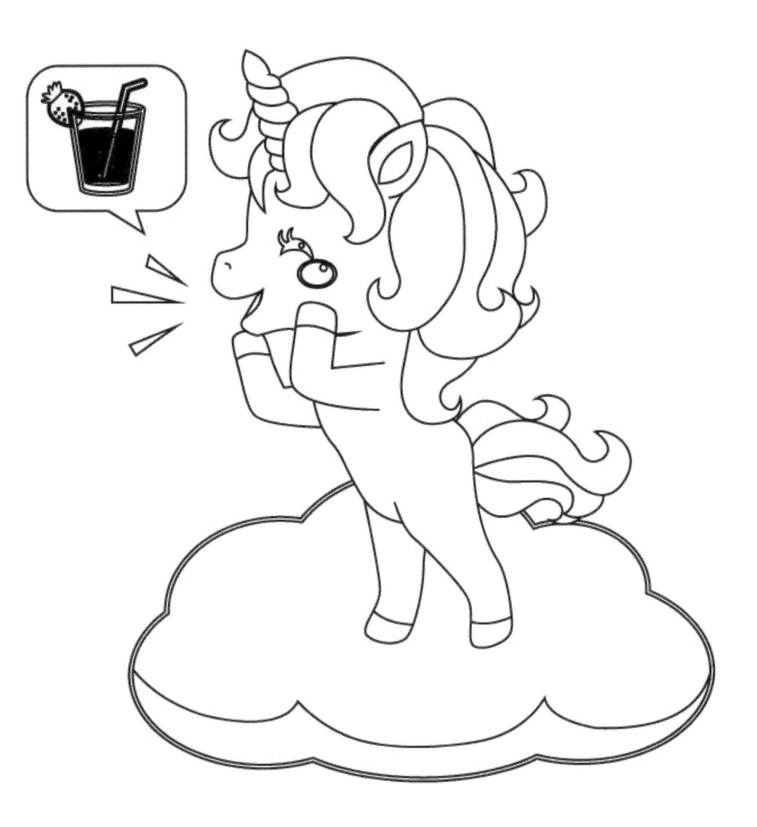

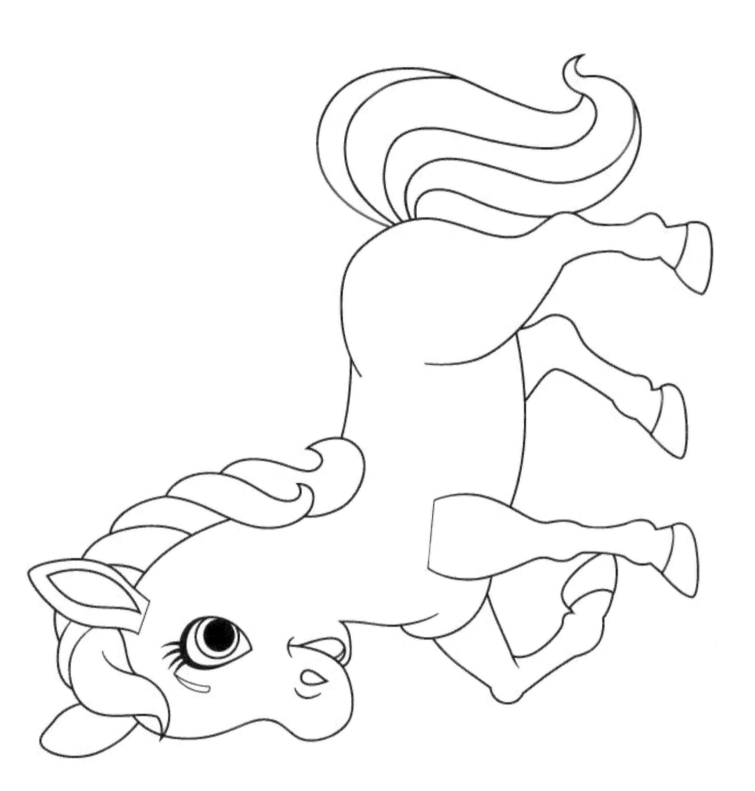

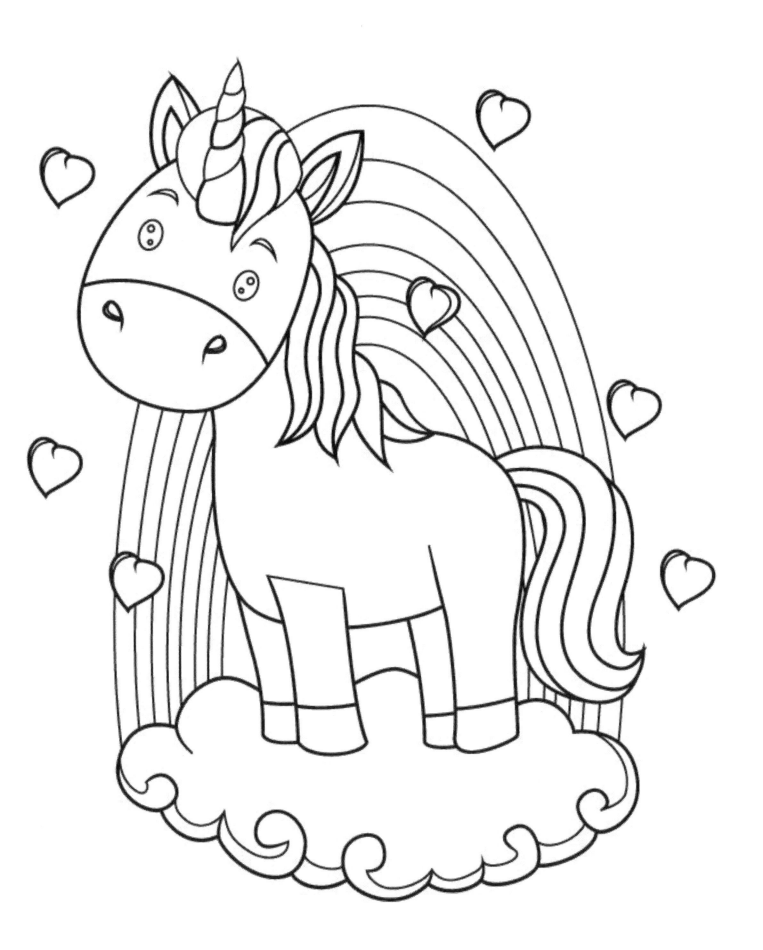

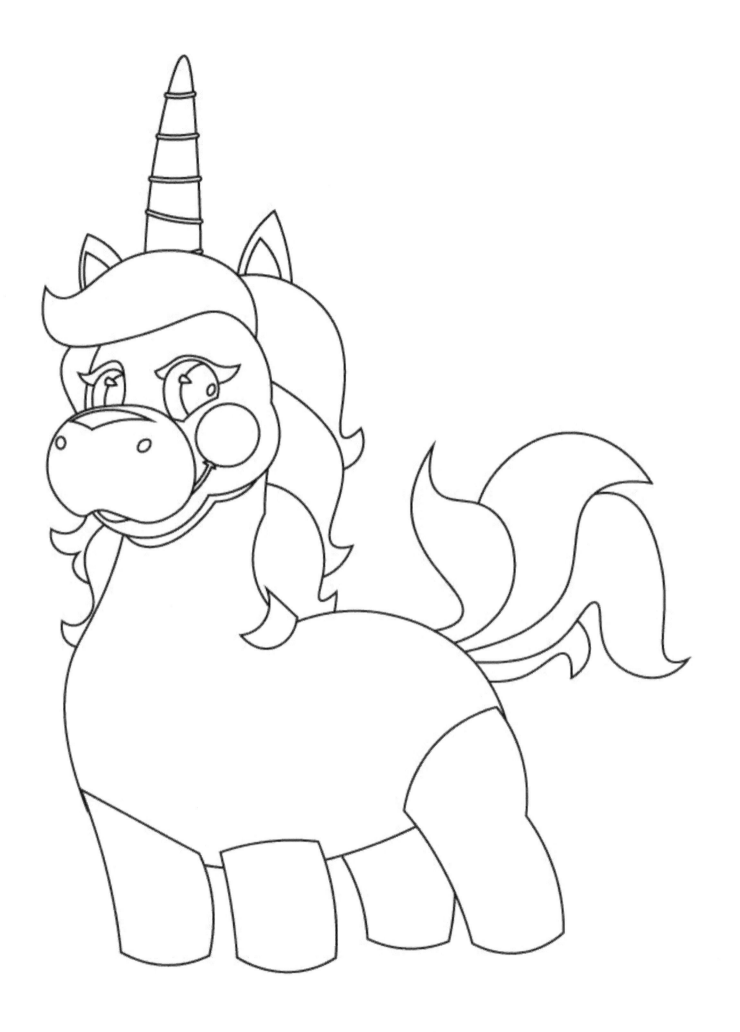

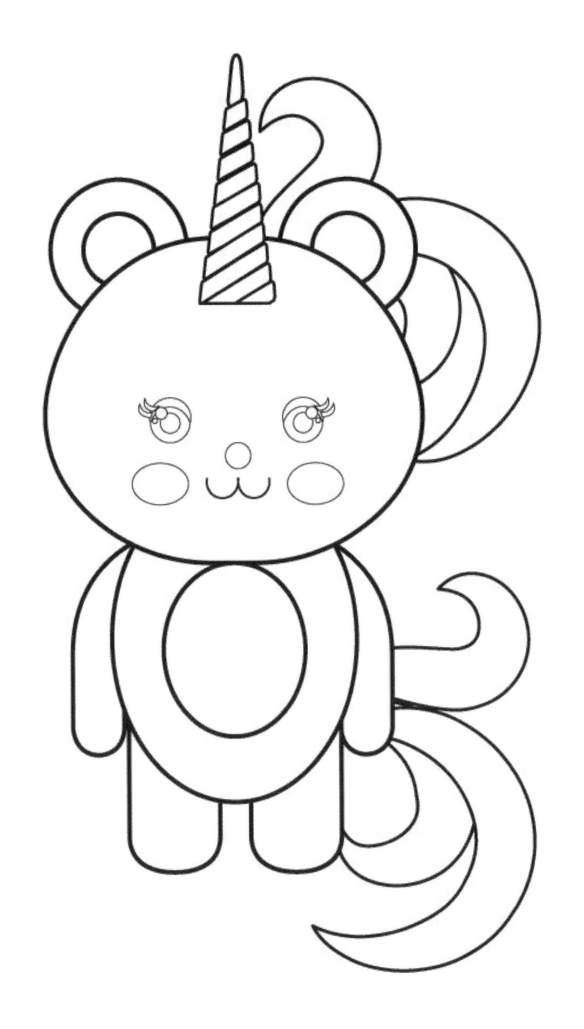

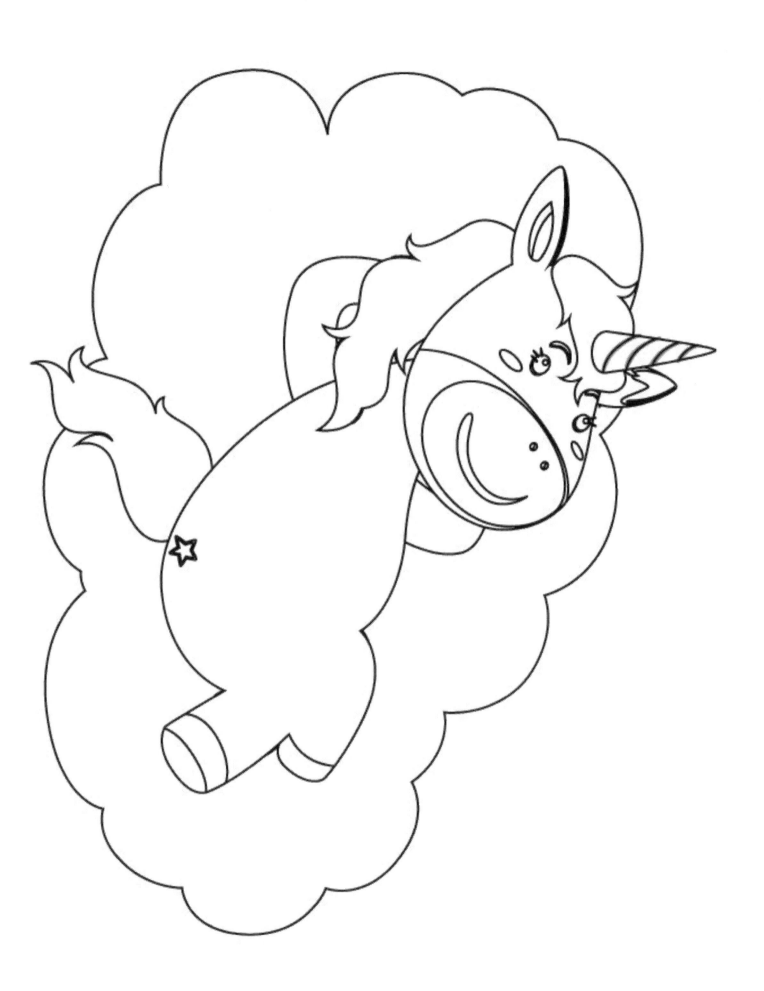

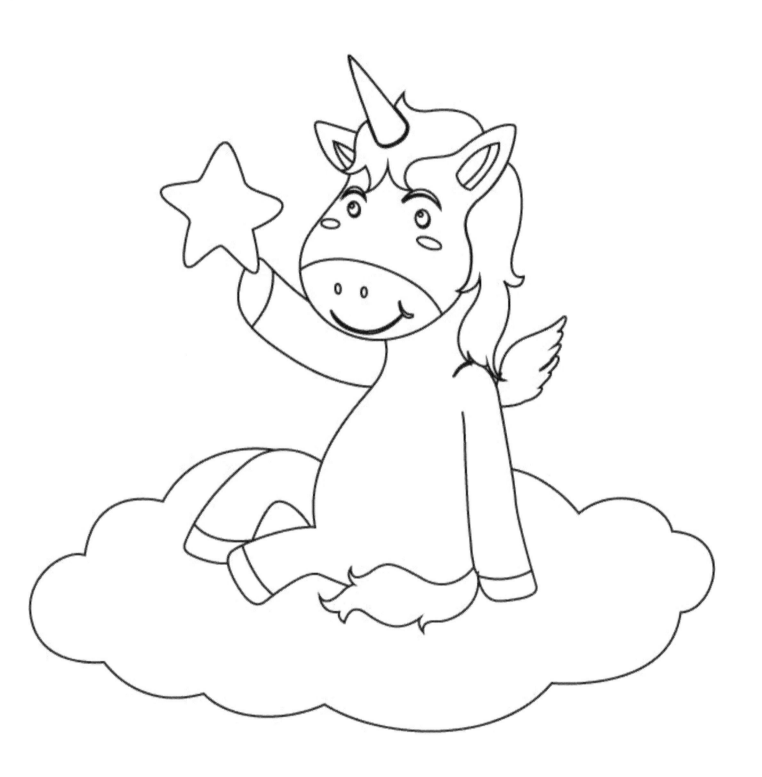

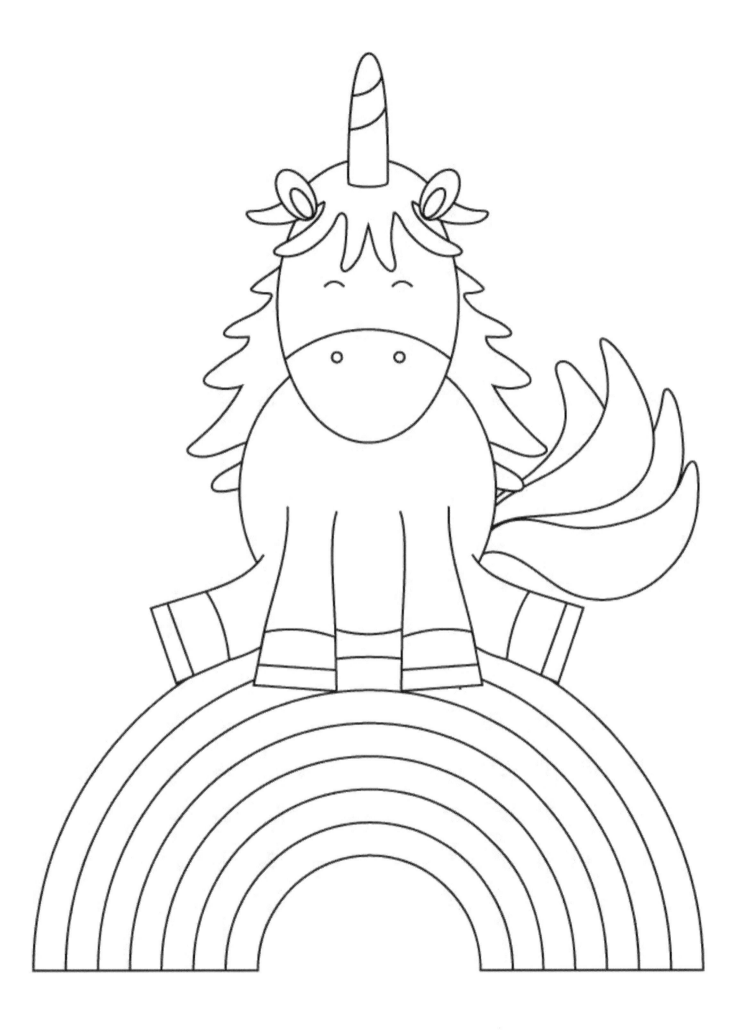

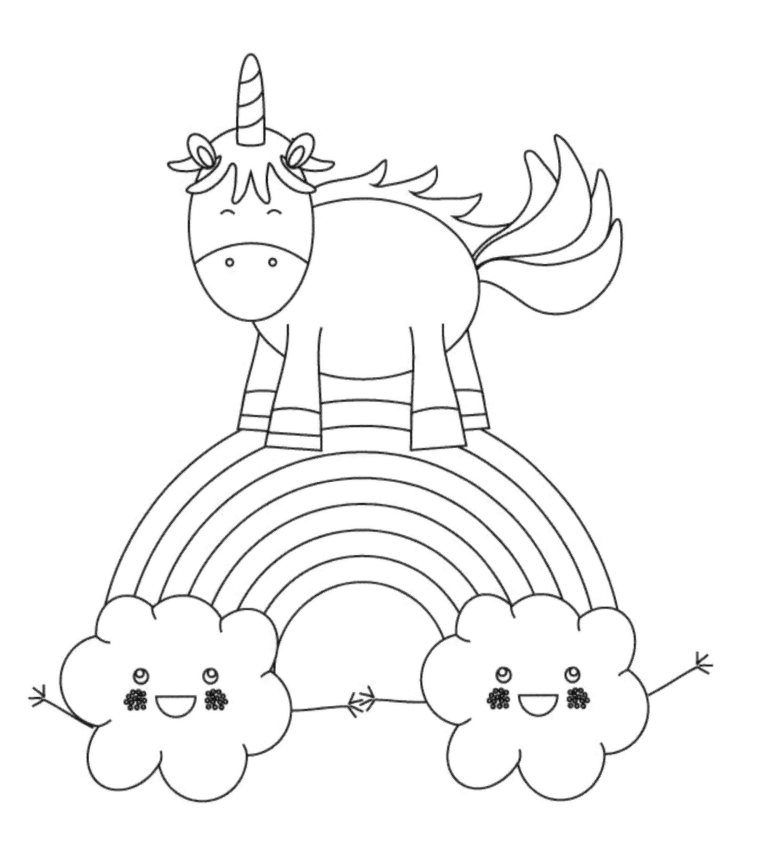

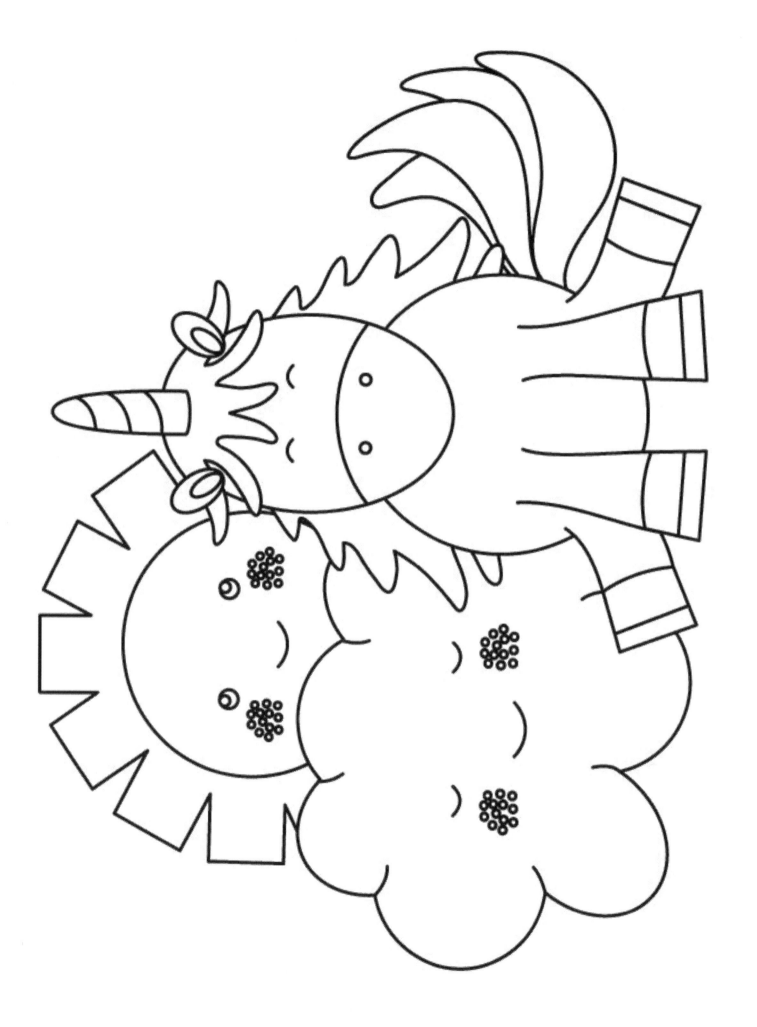

Hope you enjoy this Unicorn
Coloring Book.

Thank you.

40692028R00031